MANHATTAN

MANHATTAN

Joseph B. Brignolo

SKYLINE
PRESS

For Larry Fried, A.S.M.P., T.I.B.

My thanks to the people of Manhattan.
J.B.B.

Produced by Boulton Publishing Services, Inc., Toronto
Designed by Fortunato Aglialoro

©1986 Oxford University Press (Canadian Branch)
SKYLINE PRESS is a registered imprint of the Oxford University Press

ISBN 0-19-540633-8
1 2 3 4-9 8 7 6
Printed in Hong Kong by Scanner Art Services, Inc., Toronto

INTRODUCTION

The Scandinavian theory has it that the intrepid Vikings were the first immigrants to this island of Manhattan. Be that as it may, recorded history tells us that the Florentine Giovanni da Verrazzano, sailing for the French King Francis I in the 100-ton three-masted vessel *Dauphine*, was the first to drop anchor in what is now New York Harbor. Verrazzano never set foot on the island but stayed on deck, watching the Indians glide by in their birch-bark canoes while his crew made soundings.

For almost another 100 years the island was inhabited solely by Indians. In 1609, the English navigator Henry Hudson, in the 800-foot twin-masted *Half Moon*, flying the blue, white and orange flag of the Dutch East India Company, sailed up the river that now bears his name, leading the way for Dutch and English colonization.

So early did invasion and immigration set the stage on this polyglot island for future generations. The Italians, French, Dutch and English gave way to a heritage of multi-racial adventurers who vitalized Manhattan. These were families looking for freedom, families who had been shackled in their own countries and who needed a new place to fulfil their ambitions.

George Washington crowned the quest for freedom with the victory of the Revolution. With new-found freedom, Manhattan traders and ship-owners planned a business revival that eventually made Manhattan into not only the largest city in America but the commercial and financial center of the world. The dream continues. Still sparked by immigrants, now from the four corners of the world, the opportunities in the city are unlimited.

South Street Seaport is a reflection of the great age of sail, when the crowded harbor was a sea of masts and rigging. In 1784 a little ship, the *Empress of China*, left her slip on the East River for a trading opportunity half-way around the world to the unfamiliar shores of China. She returned 15 months later with a substantial profit, not to mention 18,000 miles of sailing experience. This venture inspired the merchant seamen and traders of Manhattan.

Today our adventurers stream through the Lincoln Tunnel, 20 million vehicles a year flooding midtown with 'sky's-the-limit' ambition, filling floors like those in the Empire State Building, for years the world's tallest. They fill the World Trade Center with 50,000 industrious workers daily (who might in their off-time string balloons on a Central Park lamp-post to celebrate the 3.5 mile Corporate Challenge).

Or it might be like the *Tight Rope Walker* statue, akin to the great adventures of men such as Wild Bill Donovan who founded and operated the O.S.S. during World War II, eventually fashioning it into the present-day C.I.A. Such great men were the offspring of immigrant forefathers, many of whom came through Castle Garden at the rate of 7,000 per day, or as latter-day migrants crowded Ellis Island on their way to the land of opportunity. They had ideas and they saw the possibilities inherent in the problems and they built the answers, like 17 daily passenger-ferries between Manhattan and Brooklyn, before the world's first suspension-bridge took their place. Answers like Trinity Church, to give thanks in for this new and vital land. Answers like the United Nations, to make it all come together for all people.

They were men who invested in our future with confidence and foresight, making the world we live in as comfortable and attractive as possible—like bringing a bit of ecology to the terraced ramparts of Park Avenue.

Their descendants stream across the George Washington Bridge, with 14 lanes of more traffic than any other bridge in the world, to work and play in the most vital city that ever existed. Some will overnight in the old-world comfort of a luxury hotel, like the Sherry Netherlands for example, for an easy night and a fresh morning start close to their next appointment. Then maybe finish up the day in a Hansom Cab for a change of pace through the vast open grounds of Central Park.

Meanwhile fast-action bike-couriers speed through traffic with documented letters, legal papers, layouts and all manner of rushes. Almost everything in this city is a rush. Except perhaps for those who are greeted with a jazz concert at City Hall on lunch hour. Perhaps in the evening there will be a chance to soak up a little culture at Lincoln Center, where the performance may be a favorite opera or a new production of Handel's *Samson* by the resident company at the Metropolitan Opera House.

Weekends in the city can be very quiet (maybe that's what we all need after a hectic week). Perhaps some meditation is in order. What better place than St. Patrick's Cathedral on Fifth Avenue—Saturday, Sunday or any day during the week. No matter which day you go you're bound to find good company.

Sculptures sprinkled inside and outside our buildings confirm the culture of most Manhattan university campuses, and at the new AT&T Madison Avenue headquarters where they finally brought *Golden Boy* down to earth, standing high and handsome in the lobby to be admired by all, and, in the North Garden of the U.N., where the Russian sculpture stands *Beating Swords into Ploughshares*.

We know for sure what George Washington intended when he was inaugurated as the country's first President here on the steps of the renamed Federal Hall, for we enjoy the fruit of his life-long labors. It comes back to us now when we see his statue, sculpted by J.Q.A. Ward in 1883, standing in about the same place where Washington took his oath of office. Thanks to his action we now have the freedom to think and do as we see fit, and to let other people know our needs—if it means putting signs on our backs like Sari Davis did in the Central Park race; the bottom line being that she too found what she wanted.

When I lived in midtown, walking to work was a pleasure. Of course there were those mornings, after not too much sleep, when you felt out of it. But even on those mornings, during the first part of the walk, I could sense the pulse of the city pumping adrenalin through me and in a matter of minutes I felt great. Now if I could have passed my Madison Avenue office and continued on to Fifth Avenue shopping I would have felt even better. Or farther up the avenue where the swirling architecture of the Guggenheim Museum lets the viewer take his course. (In this case, *her* course, as Liu Ping fresh from Beijing matches cultures.)

Little Italy with its concentrated selection of ethnic restaurants deserves at least four hours for dinner. You can come as you are, dressed perhaps in clothes designed and made right up the street in the garment district where some of America's top designers are wrapped in their international reputations.

Down the block Chinatown opens up like no other town during the Chinese New Year. Ta-Fong prepares his Centre Street temple with flowers, fruits and colorful lights decorating the statues of Buddha. The whole effect looks like the entrance to heaven. Tomorrow, hordes of Buddhists will come in for his blessing and a clean start for the new year.

Ed Koch, one of New York's most popular mayors since Fiorello La Guardia, is very visible handling the action on the city scene and still takes time out to congratulate the winners and console the losers in his inimitable way. You can bet the Mayor has had more than one egg cream to cool him off, as the local political scene can get pretty hot. But not as hot as peak rush-hour in Penn Station.

If you're lucky you might see the lithe figure of Frances Raines at Penn Station on her way to make her 13th movie. If it's the weekend, she could be at Central Park letting the wind work the bubble-pipe into a frenzy. Had she been from an earlier time I wouldn't be surprised to see Diamond Jim slip one of Tiffany's finest on her artistic finger. (There weren't many entrepreneurs as talented as Charles Lewis Tiffany whose first day's receipts totaled $4.98 and who 63 years later left an estate worth $35 million.)

But most of us, no matter who we are, no matter where we live, have seen America's favorite, the *Statue of Liberty*. Her torch signifies the liberty associated with our country and above all the very life style of *Manhattan*.

1 (*right*) 'The Street of Ships' as South Street Seaport was called in the 19th century at the peak of Manhattan's maritime history. Now the *Andrew Fletcher* paddlewheeler, built in the old style, casts off with an excursion of tourists.

2 Manhattan is a celebration every day of the year. It could be on Broadway or in Bloomies, the Coliseum or the Garden, but this one is in Central Park, celebrating with clusters of balloons the beginning of the Third Corporate Challenge 3.5 Mile Race.

3 With the Empire State Building as a background the Lincoln Tunnel turn-out, world's only tube with three tunnels of traffic, handles close to 20 million vehicles a year, under the Hudson River between New Jersey and Manhattan.

4 The history of lower Broadway lives
side by side with St. Paul's Chapel.
Completed in 1766, it is Manhattan's
oldest public building, at the foot of the
Port Authority's twin-towered World
Trade Center, that houses a working
population of 50,000 people plus another
80,000 tourists every day.

5 The elegant poise of the *Tight Rope Walker* by Kees Verkade, on the campus of Columbia University, is synonymous with the life-style of General William J. (Wild Bill) Donovan, founder and director of the O.S.S. and father of the present C.I.A. Donovan was a graduate of Columbia, and the statue was donated by his friends.

6 The hope and anguish are clear in this vignette of *The Immigrant* statue in Battery Park. Dedicated to the 7.6 million people of all nations who entered America through Castle Garden between 1855 and 1890.

7 (*right*) Cornelius Vanderbilt established the Staten Island Ferry in 1817 with his first ship, *Nautilus*. Later in 1890 the fare started at five cents for the five-mile ride. Today ferries leave every 15 minutes during peak rush hours, carrying 70,000 commuters daily, and the cost is only a quarter!

8 (*left*) The Brooklyn Bridge was inaugurated in 1883, replacing a fleet of 17 ferries that connected lower Manhattan with what was once the independent City of Brooklyn. It was the first steel-suspension spanned-bridge, set with a web of cables that spawned a thousand Big Apple legends.

9 "Let Us Beat Our Swords Into Ploughshares" is what the United Nations is all about. Sculpted by Evgeniy Vuchetich, this statue of peace was a gift of the Soviet Union and today stands in the north garden of the U.N.

10 (*left*) On lower Broadway, facing Wall Street, stands the present Trinity Church, completed in 1846. It was the third church built on the same site. The original, established in 1697 by Royal Charter of King William III of England, was destroyed by the Great Fire. The second died of structural failures.

11 Park Avenue Investments are bullish on this lush, planted terrace overlooking Park Avenue. The investment company's well-manicured roof-garden, conveniently outside their door, tells you something about the investment business, both inside and out.

12 By George! Over 46 million vehicles yearly make the east-bound pilgrimage over the world's only 14-lane suspension bridge. The Jersey connection over the Hudson River to Manhattan's West 178th Street was once to be granite-clad, but the public preferred the bare, strong, steel look of the George Washington Bridge.

13 The slender European-style clock
tower of the Sherry Netherlands Hotel
looks out through high-arched windows
from Fifth Avenue. Awninged windows
and flags fly along Central Park South,
which sets off the landmark tower.

14 Delicate looking wrought-iron bridges lace over some of the four miles of bridle-paths that wind through tree-covered Central Park, giving the riders that country look.

15 (*right*) Manhattan's fastest traffic threader, ridden by two wheeled daredevils, slashes through traffic, making quick deliveries. If you ever have the chance to question one of these delivery boys, the answer will probably be, "It's the only way, man."

16 Listening to noon-time jazz on the steps of City Hall helps you cope with the hustle and bustle of city life. Just a half-hour of mellow music guarantees to relax you for what's coming.

17 (*right*) When the patrons of Lincoln Center's New York State Theater file out for intermission, they pause in pleasant surroundings. Perhaps they were enjoying Donizetti's *Daughter of the Regiment*, performed by the resident company, the New York City Opera, whose director is Beverly Sills.

18 Like a guardian angel, St. Patrick's Cathedral hovers over Fifth Avenue with her slender spires reaching heavenward. She is mid-town's favorite religious center. All denominations seem to respond to her classic Gothic design.

19 The *Pyramid Butterfly* sculpture, practically kaleidoscopic in color, seems to create a tranquil atmosphere for these two prospective students, who are taking time to consider the courses for their Fall semester at Fordham University's Manhattan campus.

20 *The Spirit of Communication* can finally be seen face-to-face in the lobby of AT&T's new Madison Avenue headquarters. The famed 24-foot bronze statue, known as *Golden Boy*, created by Evelyn Beatrice Longman, spent the last 64 years atop AT&T's lower Broadway headquarters.

21 Works of the world's most eminent artists were commissioned by the World Trade Center to enhance their already spectacular property. Experience Alexander Calder's *Stabile* and perhaps you will feel the space-like sculpture may not linger long on the corner of Church and Vessey Streets.

22 This larger-than-life statue of George Washington stands on the steps of America's first capital building, Federal Hall. This is the same spot where Washington was inaugurated on April 30, 1789 as the first president of the United States.

23 Innovation is an American trademark, and Sari Davis employs it to her own end on a subject that vexes most Manhattanites—finding a place to live. Her friend Marcia Kline puts the finishing touches on Sari's sign and wears one just like it. Did she get a new apartment? You bet she did!

24 (*left*) Winding up like a pro, Constance Nancy Brown, pitcher for Tom Murray's *Hudson Bay Grizzlies*, throws a fast ball that's not easy for the opposition to deal with—because she's been doing it since kindergarten.

25 Looking down East 42nd Street at sunset, catching the homeward-bound streams of traffic merge into midtown, as the lighted art-deco crown of the Chrysler Building watches over all from above.

26 Whatever is chic is happening on Fifth Avenue—the most exclusive hotels and clubs, the fashionable churches, and as for retail shopping a Fifth Avenue label represents the best taste in America.

27 Atop the 77-foot granite column stands the marble statue of Christopher Columbus, who at this point can oversee the whole of Columbus Circle. He can look down Broadway, wait for the next show at the Coliseum, or amuse himself with the action in Central Park.

29 The genius of Frank Lloyd Wright's simplicity of design and function flows through the Guggenheim Museum as an art-work in its own right. Superimposed like a masterful matrix is the silhouette of China's Liu Ping.

28 (*left*) Looking like a French Renaissance chateau inside and out, the famed Westin Plaza Hotel holds court on the most impressive corner in Manhattan, Fifth Avenue and Central Park South. When opened in 1907, the extravagant room rate was $2.50 a night. We won't talk about today's rate; but one thing for sure—you'll get your money's worth.

30 (*left*) The rigging of the four-masted bark *Peking* once carried over an acre of sail as she knifed her way through the high seas. Now she is docked at the South Street Seaport, in juxtaposition with the sleek glass-clad Continental Insurance Building at 180 Maiden Lane.

31 Cooling off on a summer weekend in Harlem can best be done at the giant Jefferson Pool on First Avenue. If you've had one of those days—come on in, the fun has just begun.

32 (*left*) The West Side Highway might be quicker but the *Day Line Hudson River* cruise gets all the kinks out. By the time you return to Manhattan from Bear Mountain, West Point and Poughkeepsie, you'll be ready to take on the city again.

33 If the Florentine Verrazzano could come across on the Staten Island Ferry now, this is what he would see, and for only a quarter! He would be looking at the reason why Manhattan is the financial and commercial center of the world.

34 *(left)* From Fifth Avenue a 200-foot-long pedestrian passage leads to the flag-decked promenade bordering the lower plaza of Rockefeller Plaza. At lunch-time tourists mix with brown-baggers on the promenade's outdoor benches.

35 *Capuzela*, or half a sheep-head, is the specialty at Puglia Italian Restaurant, nestled on Hester Street in the heart of Little Italy. The colors of the Italian flag are worn with pride.

36 (*left*) Three out of four ready-made dresses and coats and four out of five fur garments are made here in the city's mid-town garment district. Trucks crowd the curbs, so bolts of fabric can be unloaded while at the same time, right down the same street, earlier bolts, now finished garments, are being loaded into more trucks.

37 From midnight till 8 a.m., for the past 163 years, fresh fish has been for sale at the Fulton Fish Market. It's still in full swing on the perimeter of South Street Seaport, living in harmony only because when one opens the other is closing.

38 (*left*) The 'East River' is a misnomer. Actually it's a tidal strait connecting the Upper Bay with Long Island Sound. Nevertheless it is affectionately known as the East River to all us city folk. In 1784, out of an East River slip, the *Empress of China* sailed on a 15-month, 18,000-mile successful trading voyage to China.

39 The easily-worked brownstone houses appeared by the hundreds in the late 19th century. By the end of the century brownstones built in the West Eighties were each built singly with a 20- or 25-foot frontage and adapted to prevailing architectural fashion. But here on West 85th Street only the best are left.

40 With its direct connection to Brooklyn's Flatbush Avenue the Manhattan Bridge, opened in 1909, with its four lanes of motor-vehicle traffic, plus several subway lines, became the busiest bridge in the city. It still carries its share among the three lower Manhattan bridges.

41 (*right*) Luciano Pavarotti in concert at Avery Fisher Hall, or the works of Balanchine performed by the New York City Ballet at the New York State Theater, and of course the world famed Metropolitan Opera House, offering the new production of Handel's *Samson*—all this and much more at the city's cultural hub, Lincoln Center.

42 The Metropolitan Museum of Art's exhibition can satisfy your innermost curiosity, can pry into the past and put history before your eyes, as in this magnificent 42,000-square-foot Michael C. Rockefeller Wing, filled with diversified groups of primitive art.

43 (*right*) Michael Heizer's 16 × 115 foot *Dragged Mass Geometric* was exhibited in 1985 at the Whitney Museum of American Art, which is devoted to the art of our country from colonial times to the present, focusing on the 20th century and living artists.

44 (*left*) The Aircraft Carrier *Intrepid* is a floating museum and a shrine to the United States Navy during World War II. Sighting down her 900-foot steel flight-deck you can almost hear the Japanese Kamikazi's making four direct hits, but she survived so that her planes could sink the super battleships, *Musashi* and *Yamato*, plus 650 enemy planes and 290 ships either sunk or damaged.

45 Only a third of a mile long, the Wall street canyon, the country's financial capital, empties out on Broadway facing the straight-laced Trinity Episcopal Church, one of the city's oldest and most famous landmarks. Perhaps the right place to go after the closing bell of the Stock Market.

46 Edward I. Koch, 105th Mayor of the City of New York, loved by just
about everyone, is known for his brevity and candor and, like a true
New Yorker, tells it like it is, like it or not!

47 Breakdancing, the most popular form of free outdoor street-
entertainment, helped into prominence by Michael Jackson, can be seen
at Fifth Avenue and 58th Street, at the Grand Army Plaza, every night of
the year, summer and winter.

48 (*left*) Clinton Street tenements, just at the end of the Williamsburg Bridge, blare with the beat of Latin music for today's Dominican, Puerto Rican and Cuban immigrants. At the corner newsstand you can buy five newspapers in English and six in Spanish.

49 A Central Park picnic, away from it all, just you and I. No traffic, no horns, no crowds or hustle-bustle, just a patch of park, quiet and green, with clean air and time to breathe it in.

New York Egg Cream

50 (*left*) To prevent monopoly of sales by auctioneers the New York stock-brokers and merchants made an agreement on May 17, 1792 to collect minimum commissions on all sales of public stock and to give preference to each other. This laid the foundation for the New York Stock Exchange as we know it today.

51 Ask anyone outside the City for an egg cream and chances are the answer will be, never heard of it! A little chocolate syrup, milk and seltzer, no straws please. A New York summer's best thirst-quencher.

52 In Chinatown, the Venerable Ta-Fong, head monk of the Centre Street Temple, prepares for Chinese New Year. According to the lunar calendar 1986 is the Year of the Tiger, symbolizing authority, power and the courage to carry on.

53 Eight hundred and forty acres of snow-covered park are perfect for a brisk, invigorating walk. And when the walk comes to an end, at Central Park South, there is any number of chic bars, in almost every direction, to warm oneself both inside and out.

54 (*left*) If you don't feel like walking, a Hansom Cab will do very nicely. Lean back, enjoy the isolation, and listen to the 'cloppity clop' and reminisce about the past—or anything, from how all this started to what's what in your own life. Central Park is the place to try it.

55 The crush of commuters passes through Penn Station by the thousand on a home-to-office pendulum via train and subway, ever since 1910. The world's busiest railroad station has Madison Square Garden Sports Complex towering above, giving you the option of which crush you would like to be entertained by.

56 (*left*) Nicknamed 'Leaping Looie' by his detractors, Paul Manship's great bronze figure of *Prometheus* is nonetheless the focal point of the lower plaza in Rockefeller Center and the recipient of more flash photos than anything else in the Center.

57 The Canal Street weekend flea-market, bordering between Soho and Chinatown, is a haven for book and record enthusiasts. You can also buy whatever you want to decorate either yourself or your home.

58 Sandwiches *al fresco* and colorful daylilies in the Trinity Church Cemetery, amid illustrious monuments of the past to Alexander Hamilton, Robert Fulton and Capt. James Lawrence, whose dying command, "Don't give up the ship," will live forever in our history. The Gothic-style Martyrs Monument to our Revolutionary heroes makes an easy landmark for meetings.

59 The sixty-foot-wide channel from Fifth Avenue is a breathtaking approach to Rockefeller Center's giant Christmas tree which stands in front of the soaring tower of 30 Rockefeller Plaza, the focal point of the 12 buildings that comprise the Center.

60 (*left*) The serenity of lunchtime concerts held in St. Paul's Chapel attracts a healthy number of visitors from the surrounding financial district. The architect Thomas McBean was probably a pupil of James Gibbs, and this could account for a resemblance to the Renaissance church of St. Martin's-in-the-Fields in London.

61 What can these three men be doing, way up on top of this granite, Gothic-styled tower of the Brooklyn Bridge, at sunset? Because it's considered to be one of the most beautiful bridges in the world, most people will be looking at the intricate webbing of cables, and not even see the trio above them.

62 (*left*) The RCA Building, in the crush of clustered midtown skyscrapers, is the focal point of Rockefeller Center. This photo was taken during a cold winter sunset from the roof of the General Motors Building.

63 The female line-up for the start of the 3.5-mile race of the Manufacturers Corporate Challenge, held in Central Park. These ready-or-not ladies are a part of the total ten thousand or more female and male competitors waiting for the action to begin at 7 p.m. on a cool summer evening.

65 Looking south along the Hudson River at sunset, with the World Trade Center's twin towers fused together from this angle, we know that the day is about to end—and the traffic is about to begin.

64 (*left*) Tree-lined Riverside Drive, like Wall Street, has always been considered a national symbol of wealth. Built during the later part of the last century, most of the mansions, hotels and apartments are still standing.

66 (*left*) When the child asked Tami, the face painter, to paint something on her face, Tami's mental process engaged, transmitting ideas and talent through her finger tips, and out came this little design on the child's cheek. On looking in the mirror the child exclaimed in surprise, how did you know? Tami knew!

67 This sculptured relief, symbolizing the working men and women of the city, graces the entrance to 640 Fifth Avenue which is actually around the corner on West 51st Street. This is not an unusual situation, as a good address comes at a premium, especially on Fifth Avenue.

68 On the sidewalk, on the south side of the Time & Life Building, lunch
wagons satisfy the need for a quick bite and some fresh air and
conversation. Greek kebabs, Mid-East falafel, Chinese noodles, Italian
sausage, as well as franks, hamburgers and icy drinks are all available
from these street vendors.

69 The Green Market at Union Square and 14th Street in its 11th season is still going strong, offering fresh produce, baked goods, fresh meats and a fishmonger, in an effort not only to serve the local residents but also to revitalize the inner city.

70 (*left*) In the early 1900's the dream-store was made a reality, by combining the merchant expertise of Bernard Gimble and Horace Saks in creating the most fashionable department store, Saks Fifth Avenue. Forty-one fashion-specialty-stores later the dream continues.

71 Manhattan is a vertical city and Trump Tower encompasses a vertical shopping center that escalates up six stories, sheathed in Breccia Perniche marble, topped by hanging gardens, with a cascading waterfall that soothes the pocketbooks after shopping in the world's most prestigious boutiques.

72 Looking straight down 50 stories, from the cold, snow-capped roof of the General Motors building, to where the blur of Madison Avenue traffic divides the heart of Manhattan, with the slanted Citicorp Tower and the Chrysler Building on the left, followed by the red-topped Empire State, and farther back the World Trade twin-towers on the right.

73 Making up one's mind for the coming attractions of the Metropolitan Opera House is no easy task, but once inside you can enter a world where dreams come true to the sound of music.

74 Knowledge is everything, especially if you can find room to concentrate on a campus that accommodates 25,500 students. Here at Columbia University there are 5,750 courses to choose from, so don't take too much time to make up your mind.

75 It's not only the stability of her architecture but also the large number of corporate headquarters ensconced along Park Avenue that enhance her reputation. The old New York Central Railroad Building, now the Hemsley, straddles the Avenue, standing in front of the Pan Am Building, built on the air-rights over Grand Central Station.

76 (*left*) Facing on the Avenue of the Americas, Radio City Music Hall, with its fabulous art-deco interior, is the home of the world-famous *Rockettes* and is the largest indoor theater in the world, seating 6,200 patrons.

77 The Museum of Natural History on Central Park West is devoted primarily to natural science exhibits and the Hayden Planetarium. Research labs, a school of advanced studies, a publishing house for scientific manuscripts, and an agency for field-exploration expeditions comprise the rest of the complex.

78 (*left*) Summer in Central Park on a warm Sunday afternoon is for making bubbles and goofing off before a hectic Monday morning is upon us. Frances Raines needs it more than most of us now that she's on her way to motion picture stardom.

79 Whiling away the hours in the art-filled garden of the Museum of Modern Art must have cultural overtones just by virtue of being there. Henry Moore's *Largo Torso Arch* helps to sustain the atmosphere at MOMA (which is what the museum is called by those in the know).

80 Trump Tower, Fifth Avenue's fanciest facade, is the city's tallest mixed-use residential, with 68 floors including retail and office space. Situated on Fifth Avenue's prime property between East 57th and 58th Streets, the Tower enjoys a showcase status.

81 (*right*) Known as 'the real village', Greenwich Village that is, Macdougal Street looks laid back during the daytime hours. But don't believe it; at night anything goes at the restaurants, night clubs and discos. If it's action you're looking for, here it is!

82 (left) Shubert Alley could be known as 'actors alley' during show castings. This is the heart-beat of Broadway, for the alley is surrounded by 13 playhouses. And every evening at showtime Shubert Alley comes alive.

83 Over 13 carats of Tiffany diamonds, set in an 18-carat gold necklace, tried on by model Anne-Marie Henderson. Among her predecessors in enjoying the famed Tiffany jewelry were J.P. Morgan, Diamond Jim Brady, Lillian Russell, Sarah Bernhardt, even Abraham Lincoln—who purchased a seed-pearl necklace for his wife Mary.

84 You have to practically get in line to enjoy this. At dusk New Yorkers, Jerseyites and tourists alike converge and cluster on the Hudson River side of Jersey City to enjoy one of the world's most spectacular sights, the World Trade Center.

85 (*right*) Broadway is all things to all people, here in the Times Square district. This Great White Way—the buildings belted with light bulbs spelling out the news, the lighted marquees of theaters and restaurants, they make it so bright that nighttime looks like high noon.

JVC
QUALITY AUDIO
AND VIDEO
STEVEN SPIELBERG Presents
TO
THE
A ROBERT ZEMECKIS Film
McDonald's
OPEN 24 HOURS
EMBASSY
RESTAURANT
Canon
Nikon
OLYMPUS
Pearlcorder

86 (*left*) City Hall Park was called 'the Commons' during the 18th century, when it was the northern boundary of the city and one mile from Battery Landing. Bordering Bloomingdale Road, now Broadway, on the west and the Boston Post Road, now Park Row, to the east, stands the City Hall, a homogenized mix of French Renaissance and American Colonial architecture.

87 In the shadow of the giant World Trade Center you can buy fresh fruits and herbs of all descriptions for a complete change of taste. If you don't have anything in mind, just browse around the brightly colored stalls for something to catch your eye.

88 The Flatiron Building was completed in 1902, when ladies skirts still trailed the ground. It was on 23rd Street, where Fifth Avenue and Broadway converge, a busy intersection and very windy, which attracted young voyeurs hoping for a glimpse of trim ankles—but the police would shoo them away and so it was said, 'Twenty-Three Skidoo!'

89 The Staten Island Ferry ride provides the finest view of lower
Manhattan. It's only a quarter. Take the trip for a comprehensive look at
lower Manhattan. Then remember that this is where it all began, with
Giovanni da Verrazzano, Henry Hudson, George Washington and the
millions of immigrants who followed.

90 Unquestionably the best-known statue in America stands as the sentinel in New York's upper bay. Bartholdi's *Statue of Liberty* was formally presented to the United States on July 4, 1884 in Paris, then shipped in 224 cases and dedicated by President Cleveland on October 28, 1886, on Bedloe Island where she stands today.